Artists Through the Ages

Francisco Goya

Alix Wood

WINDMILL BOOKS

New York

Published in 2013 by Windmill Books, An Imprint of Rosen Publishing
29 East 21st Street, New York, NY 10010

Editor for Alix Wood Books: Eloise Macgregor
US Editor: Sara Antill
Designer: Alix Wood

Photo Credits: Cover, 1, 29 © Joseph S. Martin - Artothek; 5 © Ramon Perez Terrassa;
7 © Artothek; 10-11 © Joseph S. Martin - Artothek; 13 © U. Edelmann, Städel Museum -
Artothek; 15 © Hans Hinz - Artothek; 16-17 © Joseph S. Martin - Artothek; 18, 19, 21, 22
© nga; 23 © Neveshkin Nikolay - Shutterstock; 25 © Artothek; 26-27 © Peter Willi -
Artothek; 3, 4, 8, 9, 28 © Shutterstock

Library of Congress Cataloging-in-Publication Data

Wood, Alix.
 Francisco Goya / by Alix Wood.
    pages cm — (Artists through the ages)
 Includes index.
 ISBN 978-1-61533-624-1 (library binding) — ISBN 978-1-61533-635-7 (pbk.) —
ISBN 978-1-61533-636-4 (6-pack)
1. Goya, Francisco, 1746–1828—Juvenile literature. 2. Artists—Spain—Biography—
Juvenile literature. I. Title.
 N7113.G68W66 2013
 759.6—dc23
 [B]
                                     2012030049

Manufactured in the United States of America

CPSIA Compliance Information: Batch #BW13WM: For Further Information contact Windmill Books, New York, New York at 1-866-478-0556

Contents

Who Was Goya?......................4

Madrid 6

Getting Noticed 8

Royal Success......................10

Monsters............................12

The Duchess of Alba 14

The Clothed Maja 16

The Peninsular War 18

Court Painter 20

The Third of May 1808 22

House of the Deaf Man 24

Black Paintings...................26

Goya's Legacy 28

Glossary...........................30

Websites...........................31

Read More and Index..................32

Who Was Goya?

Francisco José de Goya y Lucientes was a Spanish painter and printmaker. Goya was born in a village near Saragossa in Aragon, Spain on March 30, 1746. He was the middle child of five children. His father was a painter and a **gilder** of altarpieces. His mother was from a wealthy family. The family moved to Saragossa. At the age of 14, Goya became an apprentice to a local painter, José Luzán. Goya spent four years learning at Luzán's **studio**.

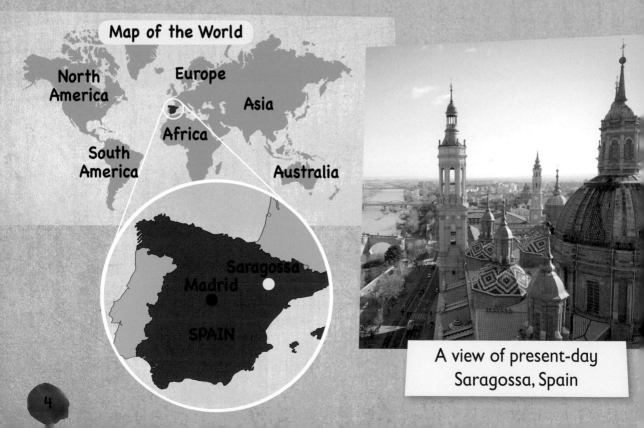

A view of present-day Saragossa, Spain

School Days

Goya went to a free school in Saragossa run by the Ignorantine Friars. The name "Ignorantine" didn't mean the teachers didn't know anything! It meant that the friar's order didn't allow any teachers with a **theological** education.

Goya's art teacher José Luzán was an accomplished but not well known Spanish painter. Like Goya, he too was the son of a painter and gilder. Luzán was made painter to the royal family by Philip V of Spain in 1741 for a short while. Luzán ran his art academy in Saragossa for many years, until bad health forced him to stop.

Goya's childhood home in Fuendetodos, near Saragossa

Madrid

Goya moved to Madrid, Spain, to study with artist Anton Raphael Mengs. They had a falling out, though, and Goya failed his examinations. He tried to enroll at the Royal Academy of Art in 1763 and 1766, but each time he was turned down. Goya made friends with the painter brothers Francisco and Ramón Bayeu y Subías and joined their studio. On July 25, 1773, Goya married their sister Josefa Bayeu. She was the niece of an **administrator** at the Royal Academy of Art. Goya reapplied after their honeymoon and was accepted!

Tapestry Designer

In 1775, Goya went to work for the Royal Tapestry Factory in Madrid. As a tapestry designer, Goya painted scenes from everyday life which the workshop would make into tapestries. Once, his design was so complicated the tapestry makers asked him to do it again. But his designs were beautiful, and he started to get private work, so he left, only to return some years later.

A tapestry design by Goya, *Boys with Mastiffs*, 1786–1787

This painting is often called *Boys with Dog* as people don't notice the second dog hiding behind the one in front. Can you see two dogs? Try counting the legs. The dogs are hunting dogs called mastiffs. They are very large!

Getting Noticed

While Goya was at the Royal Tapestry Factory he designed many tapestries which were used to decorate the bare stone walls of the newly built homes of the Spanish **monarchs** near Madrid. This brought his talent to the attention of royalty. Work in the tapestry factory stopped while Spain was at war with England, as the war took up most of the royal family's time and money.

Many of Goya's tapestries were designed to hang in this vast palace, the Royal Monastery of San Lorenzo de El Escorial, Spain.

Lost Tapestries

Though Goya was allowed to keep the color sketches for the tapestries he designed, the finished "cartoons," as they were called, became property of the king. Many cartoons Goya completed were not discovered until the late 19th century. They had been stored in rolls in the basement of the Royal Palace in Madrid.

Goya went with Francisco Bayeu to Saragossa to do a painting project together. Goya and Bayeu argued, which spoiled their friendship. Goya returned to Madrid and was asked to paint a panel of the altarpiece at the church of San Francisco el Grande. As Bayeu was also asked to paint one, Goya spent two years on his panel, making sure that it would look good next to his former friend's work.

Royal Success

His hard work on the altar panel must have impressed. His circle of **patrons** grew. They included dukes and duchesses, and even the King of Spain. In 1786, Goya was given a **salaried** position as painter to Charles III. This was the most important job for an artist in Spain. He remained court painter during the reigns of Charles IV and Ferdinand VII, too.

The Family of Charles IV of Spain, 1800–1801. Charles IV's wife, Louisa, was said to have had the real power in the family. To hint at that, Goya put her in the middle of the group portrait. Goya painted himself into the painting, too! He is at the back, on the left, in the shadows.

Monsters

Some time between late 1792 and early 1793, Goya suffered a serious illness which left him deaf. He became withdrawn. Modern doctors think that the lead in his paint was poisoning him. While recovering, he experimented with a new style. He called the series *Los Caprichos*. Goya drew about the foolishness of Spanish society. He poked fun at superstitions, the ignorance of the people in power, bad teachers, bad marriages, and religion.

The Sleep of Reason Produces Monsters is probably Goya's best known work from this time. An artist is asleep at his desk, while bats and owls fly around him, and two cats stare at him. An owl is prodding the artist with a crayon holder! Goya is showing how **irrational** a rational man's dreams can be. Goya notes that a rational man (like him) can turn the same dream into art.

Xavier

Goya and his wife had a son named Xavier. He is the only one of their 20 children to survive into adulthood.

The Sleep of Reason Produces Monsters, 1797–1798

The Duchess of Alba

The 13th Duchess of Alba was the richest woman in Spain. She was beautiful and strong-willed. The Duchess charmed Goya when they met. She asked him to put on her makeup! Goya wrote in a letter, "the Alba woman, who yesterday came to the studio to make me paint her face, and she got her way. I enjoyed it more than painting on canvas, and I still have to do a full-length portrait of her."

The Duchess of Alba's full name before she was married was María del Pilar Teresa Cayetana de Silva Alvarez de Toledo y Silva Bazán! When the Duchess of Alba's husband died she shut herself away in her house. Goya went to stay with her and painted her.

Signatures

In two of Goya's portraits of the Duchess she points at writing in the sand. This writing translates "To the Duchess of Alba, Fr. de Goya 1795." Her bracelet has Goya's initials on. In the other portrait, the writing says "Solo Goya" or "Only Goya." Some people think this signature means they were in love.

The Duchess of Alba, 1795

The Clothed Maja

Goya did two paintings of the same woman. "Maja" means an attractive working-class woman. The paintings were almost exactly the same, except in the other painting she had no clothes on!

The Spanish Inquisition

The Spanish Inquisition was a ruthless Roman Catholic court which punished people who went against the teachings of the church. Punishments ranged from public shame to being burned at the stake! Goya was brought before the Inquisition and asked who had paid him to paint the nude painting of the Maja. No one knows if he gave them an answer, but he did live to tell the tale.

The painting caused a bit of a stir in the United States in 1930, too. Two sets of stamps of *The Naked Maja* were made to celebrate Goya's work and approved by the Spanish Postal Authority. The United States government barred them, though, and returned any mail bearing the stamps!

The Clothed Maja, painted between 1797 and 1800

The Peninsular War

In 1808 war broke out in Spain. Goya visited battle sites and drew what he saw. Instead of glorifying war as artists had in the past, Goya's series of prints, *The Disasters of War*, showed the horror, the struggle, and the hunger.

And This Too, 1810–1820

The titles of Goya's pictures in this series are interesting. Some of the pictures were drawn after Goya had been told about the events, but some were scenes he had actually witnessed. One of Goya's works is called *Yo Lo Vi* (*I Saw It*), and under it on the same page is the picture on page 18, *Y Esto Tambien* (*And This Too*).

A Pause

The Disasters of War wasn't published in Goya's lifetime. Maybe Goya was afraid of the new regime. He didn't want his images used for political motives, and he didn't want them to be **censored**.

Court Painter

After the war, Goya kept his job as court painter. He had to swear an oath of loyalty to the new king first. Goya painted portraits of important people from all sides of the war. He painted Joseph Bonaparte, who was the new king of Spain and the brother of French emperor Napoleon. He painted the English Duke of Wellington and French and Spanish generals.

Goya's portraits were very realistic. Goya never flattered the sitters by making them look more attractive than they actually were. This could be a brave thing to do if your subject was a powerful king or general!

Who is the Boy?

The painting on the right is of the nephew of one of the most important French generals in Spain. Young Victor Guye wears the uniform of the Order of **Pages** to the King of Spain. At six or seven years old, he was probably too young to actually be a court page. Maybe he was allowed to wear the uniform because of how important his uncle was.

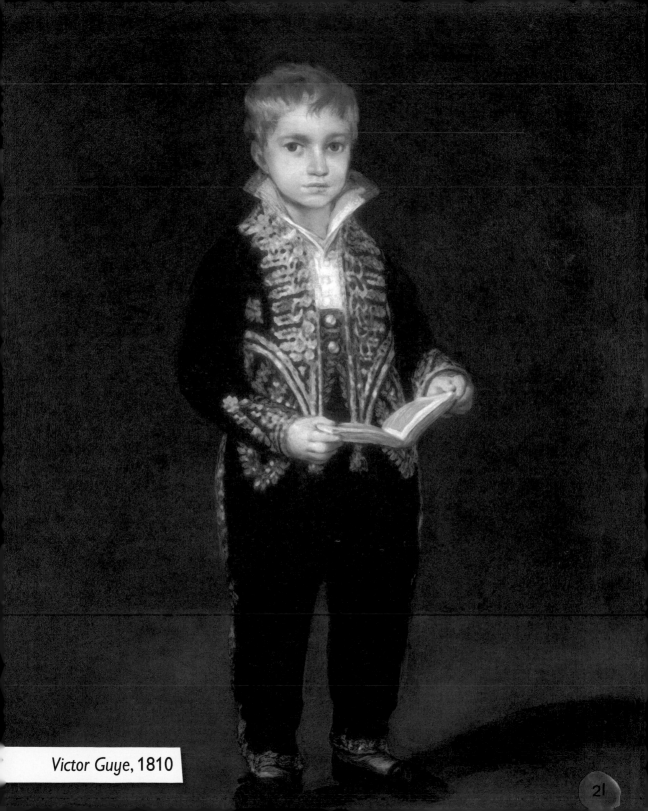

Victor Guye, 1810

The Third of May 1808

Goya commemorated the Spanish resistance during the Peninsular War in his painting *The Third of May 1808*. The painting was groundbreaking. Set in the morning following an uprising, it shows the ordered line of the French firing squad taking aim at the disorganized group of Spanish captives.

Why "Groundbreaking?"

For the first time, a painting done of people dying for a cause was not given any nobility. You can see the hopeless situation the captives are in. Goya's treatment was echoed by Édouard Manet's *The Execution of the Emperor Maximilian* (left) and Pablo Picasso's *Massacre in Korea* years later.

It is clever how Goya has lit the left side of the painting so the man in the white shirt is so bright. The soldiers are all in shadow and this makes them look dark and menacing. It is easy to see who Goya thought were the good guys!

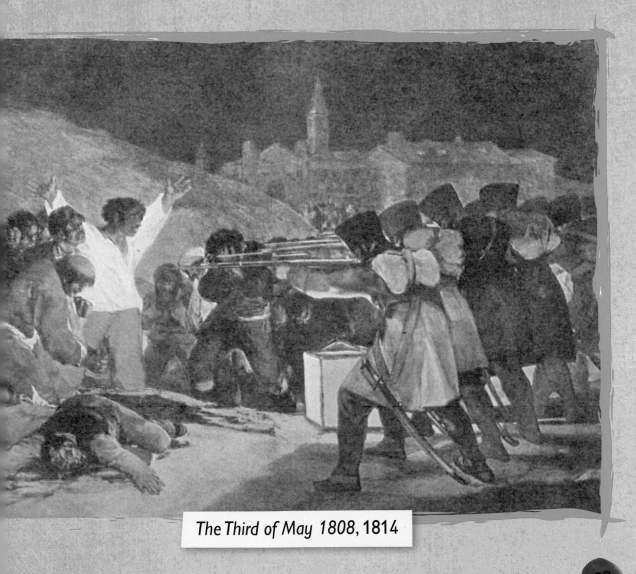

The Third of May 1808, 1814

House of the Deaf Man

In 1819, at the age of 72, Goya bought a country house just outside Madrid. It was known as the Quinta del Sordo or "House of the Deaf Man." It was actually called that after a previous owner and not because Goya was deaf. After Goya's wife, Josefa, died, he was cared for by his maid, Leocadia Weiss. She was 35 years younger than him and a distant relative. She had a daughter named Rosario. Still under threat from the Inquisition, Goya signed Quinta del Sordo over to his grandson Mariano and asked King Ferdinand if he could leave for France. He was allowed to leave and he and Leocadia settled first in Paris, and then in Bordeaux.

Photograph of Quinto del Sordo taken in 1905. The people in the picture are unknown.

The Milkmaid
of Bordeaux,
painted between
1825 and 1827

Leocadia or Rosario?

The Milkmaid of Bordeaux is thought to be of
Leocadia or her daughter Rosario. This was
the only painting Leocadia was able to keep
after Goya's death, as everything else went
to Goya's son Xavier and grandson Mariano.

Black Paintings

When Goya returned to Quinta del Sordo he continued a series of **frescoes** he was painting on to the plaster walls of the house. The series has become known as the "Black Paintings." The paintings were not meant to be seen by anybody but himself and maybe his closest friends. They are all very dark, haunting images. In 1878, years after Goya's death, the frescoes were transferred to canvas supports. The house has since been knocked down.

A *Pilgrimage to San Isidro* was one of the frescoes on Goya's walls at Quinta del Sordo.

Some scholars are not sure if the "Black Paintings" are Goya's work. When Goya gave Quinta del Sordo to his grandson, it was described in the deeds as a one story house. The frescoes were found on the walls of two stories of the building.

Horrible Subjects

Saturn Devouring His Son was another of the frescoes. It's a bit gruesome! The painting tells the story of the god Saturn who was afraid that his children would take his power from him, so he ate them all! One son, Jupiter, did escape, and he did take all Saturn's power.

Goya's Legacy

Goya died of a stroke in 1828, at the age of 82. He was buried in Bordeaux, France at the cemetery of the Chartreuse of Bordeaux. In 1919 his body was moved 344 miles (554 km) south to the Royal Chapel of St. Anthony of La Florida in Madrid, surrounded by the frescoes he had painted there. Goya is often called "the first of the moderns." He was very important to the art world. His **legacy** and influence can be seen in many modern works of art.

The Missing Head

When Goya's body was moved from Bordeaux to Madrid, his head was missing! It may have been stolen from the cemetery in Bordeaux. The study of the size and shape of skulls, called phrenology, was very popular at the time. Grave robbing was also very common. Many people may have wanted to study the skull of an artist like Goya!

A phrenology model

Self-Portrait, 1815

Glossary

administrator
(ed-MIH-neh-stray-ter)
A person who manages
the day-to-day affairs,
especially of a business,
a school, or of
government affairs.

censored (SEN-serd)
Having things deleted
that are thought to be
objectionable.

frescoes (FRES-kohz)
Paintings done on freshly
spread, moist plaster.

gilder (GILD-er)
A person who covers
objects with a coating
of gold.

irrational
(ih-RA-shuh-nul)
Something not based
on reason.

legacy (LEH-guh-see)
Something a person
leaves behind after their
death, which can be
wealth or knowledge.

monarchs
(MAH-narks)
People who reign over
a kingdom or empire.

page (PAYJ)
A young person serving
a person of rank.

patrons (PAY-trunz)
Those who give generous
support or approval.

salaried (SAL-uh-reed)
Receiving a regular wage.

studio (STOO-dee-oh)
The working place of
an artist.

theological
(thee-uh-LAH-jih-kul)
Concerning the study
of religion.

Websites

For web resources related to the
subject of this book, go to:
www.windmillbooks.com/weblinks
and select this book's title.

Read More

McNeese, Tim. *Francisco Goya*. The Great Hispanic Heritage. New York: Chelsea House, 2008.

Venezia, Mike. *Francisco Goya*. Getting to Know the World's Greatest Artists. Danbury, CT: Children's Press, 1992.

Wright, Patricia. *Goya*. Eyewitness Books. New York: DK Publishing, 2001.

Index

A
Alba, Duchess of 14
And This Too 18, 19
B
Bayeu, Josefa 6
Bonaparte, Joseph 20
Boys with Mastiffs 7
C
Charles III of Spain 10
Clothed Maja, The 16, 17
D
Disasters of War, The 18, 19
Duchess of Alba, The 15
Duke of Wellington 20

E
Execution of the Emperor Maximilian, The, 22
F
Family of Charles IV of Spain, The 10, 11
Ferdinand VII of Spain 10, 24
G
Goya, Mariano 24, 25
Goya, Xavier 12, 25
L
Los Caprichos 12
Luzán, José 4, 5
M
Manet, Édouard 22
Milkmaid of Bordeaux, The 25

P
Pilgrimage to San Isidro, A 26, 27
Q
Quinta del Sordo 24, 26, 27
S
Saragossa, Spain 4, 5, 9
Self-Portrait 29
Sleep of Reason Produces Monsters, The 12, 13
T
Third of May 1808, The 22, 23
V
Victor Guye 20, 21